Copyright © 2021 by Wiseblood Books

All rights reserved, including the right to reproduce this book or portions thereof in any form whatsoever. For information, address the publisher:

>Wiseblood Books
>P.O. Box 870
>Menomonee Falls, WI 53052

Printed in the United States of America
Set in Baskerville Typesetting

Photography: View from the South, Olvr © CC-BY-SA 3.0; West Facade, Robin Poitou © CC-BY-3.0; South Facade, Ivy Positano © CC-BY-3.0; Central Bay, Guillaume Piolle © CC-BY-3.0; Portal of North Transept, Lawrence Lew, O.P. © CC-BY-NC-ND-2.0; Statues at North Portal, Steve Zucker © CC-BY-NC-SA-2.0; Astronomical Clock, Selbymay © CC-BY-SA-3.0; Choir, Marianne Casamance © CC-BY-SA-3.0; Northern Rose Window, Guillaume Piolle, Public Domain; Crucifixion and Road to Emmaus, Lawrence Lew, O.P. © CC-BY-NC-ND-2.0; Notre-Dame de la Belle-Verrière and Wedding at Cana, Vassil, Public Domain; Behind the Cathedral, Peter Kwasniewski; Labyrinth in the Bishop's Garden, Ebe94 © CC-BY-SA 3.0
Cover Design: Silk Sheep Studio

ISBN-13: 978-1-951319-68-7

Wiseblood Books
Milwaukee, Wisconsin
www.wisebloodbooks.com

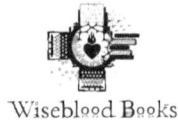

Death Comes for the Cathedrals

MARCEL PROUST

TRANSLATED AND INTRODUCED BY
DR. JOHN PEPINO

WITH AN AFTERWORD BY
DR. PETER KWASNIEWSKI

CONTENTS

Introduction by Dr. John Pepino   1

Death Comes for the Cathedrals by Marcel Proust   7

Afterword by Dr. Peter Kwasniewski   29

LIST OF PLATES

View from the South	iv
West Facade	6
South Facade	11
Central Bay	12
Portal of North Transept	12
Statues at North Portal	13
Astronomical Clock	13
Choir	24
Northern Rose Window	25
Crucifixion	26
Road to Emmaus	26
Notre-Dame de la Belle-Verrière	27
Wedding at Cana	28
Behind the Cathedral	32
Labyrinth in the Bishop's Garden	32

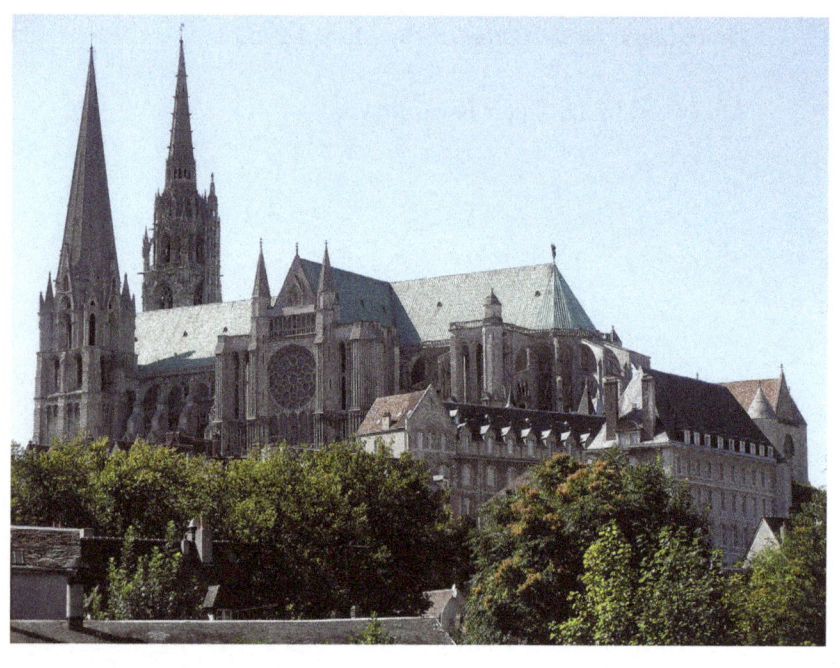

INTRODUCTION

The text we here present holds an eerie, even uneasy, relevance to our own time. Marcel Proust's 1904 warning that the forces of early-twentieth-century freethinking might (in just sixty years, it turned out) snuff out the liturgy for which the great cathedrals, indeed all the churches, of France were consecrated amounts to an uncomfortable prophecy. The lyricism with which he describes the then-threatened rites and liturgical texts makes us, in the twenty-first century, wince.

Yet Proust's piece is embedded in its own time and place: Paris of the *Belle-Époque* with its specific political, literary, and artistic flavors. It is as turn-of-the-century French as cigarettes, coffee, and Cognac; it requires some explanation.

Since the Concordat of July 15, 1801 between Napoleon I and Pope Pius VII, not only had the Catholic faith enjoyed full freedom in France, but the clergy was subsidized by the government as reparation for the seizure and sale of ecclesiastical property during the Revolution. The procedure by which bishops were named became a complex negotiation between the civil State and the Vatican, with input from the Minister of Worship, the bishops, and the Apostolic Nuncio. This had led to some friction under the increasingly anticlerical Third Republic (from 1870 on), which by the mid-1880s had secularized the cemeteries and hospitals, suppressed military chaplaincies and public prayer, and legalized divorce. The government was notoriously filled with Freemasons and had set up its public school system in part to extirpate "superstition" (here meaning religion) from town and country. It had forbidden religious orders (Jesuits, Christian Brothers, the Mesdames of the Sacred Heart, etc.) from running schools and even kicked monks and nuns out of France, *manu militari* if need be. The Dreyfus affair[1] still pitted against each other

---

1. Captain Alfred Dreyfus, a Jew, had been condemned for espionage in 1894; he would be acquitted in 1906.

"the two Frances" (viz., Catholic, monarchist, traditional against Freemasonic, republican, socialist) to use the conventional, if inadequate (there were anti-Semites on all sides) historiographical categories. In May of 1904, three months before Proust's article came out, France and the Vatican had broken off diplomatic relations over the French president's State visit to the king of Italy, Victor-Emmanuel III, whose grandfather had taken Rome from the papacy.

At the Government level, debates came to a head in 1904, when parliamentarian Aristide Briand (1862–1932), a Freemason and Republican-Socialist ("Republican" here meaning anti-monarchist and secularist), proposed his bill on the "Separation of Church and State": *le projet Briand* ("the Briand bill"). He had elaborated it as part of a commission of thirty-three men, of whom the absolute majority of seventeen were openly in favor of Separation. The president of this commission, representative Ferdinand Buisson, a self-professed "Liberal Protestant," was the president of the National Association of Freethinkers and remained famous for his political fight to secularize education; it was he who had popularized the term *laïcité*, "secularism." Some of the members—Proust mentions their schemes, which had been made public—were fanatical proponents of the actual destruction of the Church (Maurice Allard, Victor Dejeante, Albert Sarraut) and wished to see the cathedrals and churches of France turned into "Houses of the People," theaters, or job exchanges, all under the jurisdiction of a "communal counsel of social education." Briand, realizing that such an agenda might precipitate civil unrest, and aware of the need to reach some compromise with the Catholic "Rightist Bloc," was able to reduce the bill to more manageable proposals. The stormiest debates in the chamber of deputies (the French version of the House of Representatives) centered on the fourth article of the bill, regarding the fate reserved for the Church's property (including, therefore, the cathedrals). In the end, the law passed in 1905 would allow religious edifices, though the property of the State and therefore the State's responsibility when it came to large repairs, to be used by the religion for which they were built (the bill also concerned Jewish synagogues and Protestant "temples," as they are called in France)—a concession doubtless owing in some part to Proust's common-sense article. The cathedrals were saved for the worship that Proust describes. For a time.

What made Proust's article so forcible was, besides his name and his well-known lack of partisanship for a religion that was no longer his own, the customary literary talent he deployed in defending the cathedrals. Our translation has attempted to give some echo of Proust's style, but his allusions need elucidating: they form part of the force of his argument.

Proust was an artist, and was abreast of the literature on art. His source for the symbolism of liturgy and architecture was Émile Mâle, whose 1899 dissertation, published in English as *The Gothic Image: Religious Art in France of the Thirteenth Century*, was a watershed work of scholarship that taught the educated public how to appreciate medieval artistry; it won him a seat at the *Académie française* in 1927. Émile Mâle also introduced Proust to *The Rationale of the Divine Offices* by William Durandus of Mende, the thirteenth-century allegorical interpreter of the liturgy and its material supports. Furthermore, Proust had read John Ruskin, perhaps the most influential architecture and art critic of the nineteenth century; in fact, Proust was so taken by Ruskin's outlook that, with the help of his mother, he translated Ruskin's more important works into French, including "The Nature of Gothic" (part of *The Stones of Venice*, published in 1853). Such familiarity explains Proust's irony when he writes "I am well aware that Ruskin . . . ." Proust even evokes the most up-to-date and talented artist of his day, Art Nouveau glassblower and woodworker Émile Gallé, whose claim to fame was his mastery of color in both media, to praise nature's work in bringing out the color of the relief work in the choirstalls of the Amiens cathedral.

Yet Proust does not rely only on scholars and connoisseurs to defend the cathedrals and the liturgies they are meant to house. He appeals also to such notorious non-Catholics and religious skeptics as Renan and Flaubert. Ernest Renan had famously written a *Life of Jesus* (1863) that dismissed the supernatural in the Gospel accounts while Flaubert, the "martyr of style," was closer to pantheism and was an unabashed sinner. Still, each contributed his share to Proust's plea, which includes verbatim Renan's tender appreciation of his simple countrymen's (he was a Breton) singing at Vespers and Flaubert's description of Madame Bovary's Last Rites. The art to which the Briand bill as proposed would condemn the cathedrals, should they be desecrated into theaters, is not the art of the finest nineteenth-century French literature, which did appreciate the edifices and rites of the Church; they would be condemned to host such light and long-forgotten comedies as Jules Sandeau's "Mister Poirier's Son-in-Law" (*Le Gendre de M. Poirier*, 1854) or Émile Augier's "The Adventuress" (*L'Aventurière*, 1848).

When Proust calls upon André Hallays' "clever zeal" to harass and indict the Minister of Public Education and Fine Arts, Joseph Chaumié (appointed two years earlier) and his chief-of-staff Anatole de Monzie, both Republican-Socialists, along with John Labusquière, the militantly socialist member of the Paris town council, all three in favor of Separation, he is calling upon the journalist who, in a popular weekly column ("En Flânant," in *Le Journal des débats*), defended the architectural patrimony of France. The same André Hallays, as Proust recounts, had condemned those citizens of Vézelay who sought to do to their magnificent twelfth-century Cluniac monastery church, the Basilica of Saint Mary Magdalene (it boasts her relics), precisely what members of the Briand commission intended for all the cathedrals and churches of France.

Proust's verve goes so far as to invoke the most famous socialist statesmen of his day: Jean Jaurès, the founder of the French Socialist Party and well-known partisan of Separation. His plea in favor of granting workers the right to form trade unions and to strike, a plea that had much to do with his fame as an orator and as a defender of the working class, had denounced the "silence" to which the anti-strike laws condemned the salaried. Anticipating by four years an argument Chesterton would make in his *Orthodoxy*, Proust invokes a sort of "democracy of the dead" when he applies

Jaurès's "silent protest" to the humble coopers and basket weavers on the stained-glass windows, the "ancestors of the electors for whom the House [of Representatives] has such little concern."

The cathedrals of France and the traditional liturgy of the Roman rite are the spiritual patrimony of the Church; of this, there is no doubt. But what Proust is here saying, what Agatha Christie and a host of English-language non-Catholic intellectuals and artists said to Paul VI in 1971, what Chaim Potok wrote in his *Asher Lev* novels (and his own painting) on the crucifix, is this: the material, artistic, and religious aspects of Catholicism are part of the patrimony of all humanity and ought to be preserved and defended for that reason as well.

Dr. John Pepino
Feast of the Annunciation
March 25, 2021

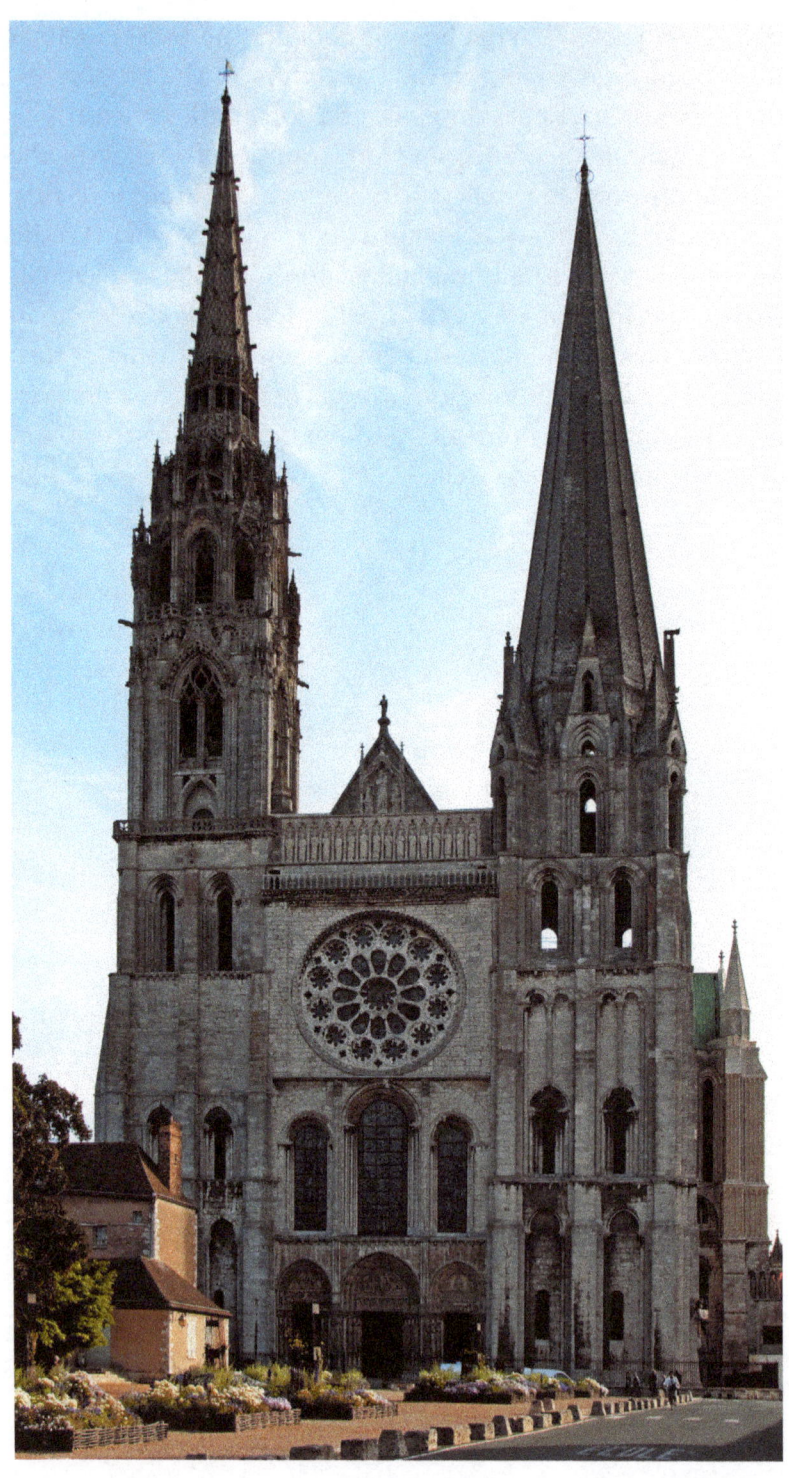

DEATH COMES FOR THE CATHEDRALS

Marcel Proust

A Consequence of the Briand Bill on the Separation of Church and State

Suppose for a moment that Catholicism had been dead for centuries, that the traditions of its worship had been lost. Only the unspeaking and forlorn cathedrals remain; they have become unintelligible yet remain admirable. Then suppose that one day scholars manage, on the basis of documentary evidence, to reconstitute the ceremonies that used to be celebrated in them, for which men had built them, which were their proper meaning and life, and without which they were now no more than a dead letter; and suppose that for one hour artists, beguiled by the dream of briefly giving life back to those great and now silent vessels, wished to restore the mysterious drama that once took place there amid chants and scents—in a word, that they were undertaking to do what the *Félibres* have done for ancient tragedies in the theater of Orange.[2]

Is there any government with the slightest concern for the artistic past of France that would not liberally subsidize so magnificent an undertaking? Do you not think that it would do what it did in the case of Roman ruins for these cathedrals, which are probably the highest, and unquestionably the most original, expression of French genius? After all, one may well prefer the literature of other peoples to ours, prefer their music to ours, their painting and sculpture to ours, but it is in France that Gothic architecture created its first and most perfect masterpieces. All that other countries have done is to imitate our religious architecture without ever matching it.

---

2. The first-century Roman theater of Orange had been restored in the nineteenth century under the aegis of the *Félibres*, a Provencal cultural association. A yearly summer theater festival (the "Chorégies") started there in 1902, two years before this article.

And so, to return to my hypothesis, here come scholars who have been able to rediscover the cathedrals' lost meaning. Sculptures and stained-glass windows recover their significance, a mysterious odor once again wafts in the temple, a sacred drama is performed, and the cathedral starts to sing once more. When the government underwrites this resurrection, it is more right to do so than when it underwrites the performances in the theaters of Orange, at the Opéra-Comique, and at the Opéra, for Catholic ceremonies have an historical, social, artistic, and musical interest whose beauty alone surpasses all that any artist has ever dreamed, and which Wagner alone was ever able to come close to, in *Parsifal*—and that by imitation.

Caravans of swells make their way to the holy city (whether it is Amiens, Chartres, Bourges, Laon, Rheims, Rouen, Paris, or whatever town you please, we have so many sublime cathedrals!), and once a year they experience the feeling they once sought in Bayreuth and in Orange: enjoying a work of art in the very setting that had been built for it. Alas, here as in Orange, they can only ever be curious dilettantes; try as they might, the soul of times past does not dwell within them. The artists who have come to perform the chants, the actors who play the role of priests may be learned, they may have imbued themselves with the spirit of the texts, and the Minister of Education will lavish medals and compliments upon them. Yet, for all that, one cannot help but think: "Alas! How much more beautiful these feasts must have been when priests celebrated the liturgy not in order to give some idea of these ceremonies to an educated audience, but because they set the same faith in their efficacy as did the artists who sculpted the Last Judgment in the west porch tympanum or who painted the stained-glass lives of the saints in the apse. How much more deeply and truly expressive the entire work must have been when a whole people responded to the priest's voice and fell to its knees as the bell rang at the elevation, not as cold and stylized extras in historical reconstructions, but because they too, like the priest, like the sculptor, *believed*. But alas, such things are as far from us as the pious enthusiasm of the Greeks at their theater performances, and our 'reconstitutions' cannot give a faithful idea of them."

That is what one would say if the Catholic religion no longer existed and if scholars had been able to rediscover its rites, if artists had tried to reproduce them for us. But the point is that it still does exist and has not really changed since the great century when the cathedrals were built. For us to imagine what a living and sublimely functioning thirteenth-century cathedral was like, we need not do with it as we do with the theater of Orange and turn it into a venue for exact yet frozen reconstitutions and retrospectives. All we need to do is to go into it at any hour of the day when a liturgical office is being celebrated. Here mimicry, psalmody, and chant are not entrusted to artists without "conviction." It is the ministers of worship themselves who celebrate, not with an aesthetic outlook, but by faith—and all the more aesthetically for that very reason. One could not hope for livelier and more sincere extras, since it is the faithful that take the trouble of unwittingly playing their role for us. One may say that thanks to the persistence of the same rites in the Catholic Church as also of Catholic belief in French hearts, cathedrals are not only the most beautiful monuments of our art, but also the only ones that still live their life fully and have remained true to the purpose for which they were built.

Now because of the French government's break with Rome, debates on M. Briand's bill and its probable passing are imminent. Its provisions indicate that after five years churches may, and often will, be shut down; the government will not only no longer underwrite the celebration of ritual ceremonies in the churches but also be habilitated to transform them into whatever it wishes: museums, conference centers, or casinos. As for you, Monsieur André Hallays! You go about repeating that works of art lose life as soon as they no longer serve the ends for which they were created, that furniture becomes so much bric-a-brac, and that a palace-turned-museum grows icy, can no longer speak to our heart, and ends up dying—I hope that you will stop for just one moment condemning the variously clumsy restorations that daily threaten the towns of France that you have taken into your care, and that you will rise to your feet, speak up, even harass Monsieur Chaumié if you have to, indict Monsieur de Monzie if need be, join Monsieur John Labusquière, and call a meeting of the Commission for Historical Monuments. Your clever zeal has often been effective; surely you will not let all the churches of France die in one fell swoop.

Today there is not one socialist endowed with taste who doesn't deplore the mutilations the Revolution visited upon our cathedrals: so many shattered statues and stained-glass windows! Well: better to ransack a church than to decommission it. As mutilated as a church may be, so long as the Mass is celebrated there, it retains at least some life. Once a church is decommissioned it dies, and though as an historical monument it may be protected from scandalous uses, it is no more than a museum. One may say to churches what Jesus said to His disciples: "Except you eat the flesh of the Son of man, and drink his blood, you shall not have life in you" (John 6:54). These somewhat mysterious yet profound words become, with this new usage, an aesthetic and architectural axiom. When the sacrifice of Christ's flesh and blood, the sacrifice of the Mass, is no longer celebrated in our churches, they will have no life left in them. Catholic liturgy and the architecture and sculpture of our cathedrals form a whole, for they stem from the same symbolism. It is a matter of common knowledge that in cathedrals there is no sculpture, however secondary it may seem, that does not have its own symbolic value. If the statue of Christ at the Western entrance of the cathedral of Amiens rests on a pedestal of roses, lilies, and vines, it is because Christ said: "I am the rose of Sharon"; "I am the lily of the valley"; "I am the true vine."[3]

If the asp and the basilisk, the lion and the dragon are sculpted beneath His feet it is because of the verse in Psalm 90: *Inculcabis super aspidem et leonem*. To His left, in a small relief, a man is represented dropping his sword at the sight of an animal while a bird continues to sing beside him. This is because "the coward hasn't the courage of a thrush": indeed the mission of this bas-relief is to symbolize cowardice, as opposed to courage, because it is set under the statue that is always (at least in earliest times) to the right of the statue of Christ, that is, under the statue of St. Peter, the Apostle of courage.

---

3. Song of Songs 2:1; John 15:1.

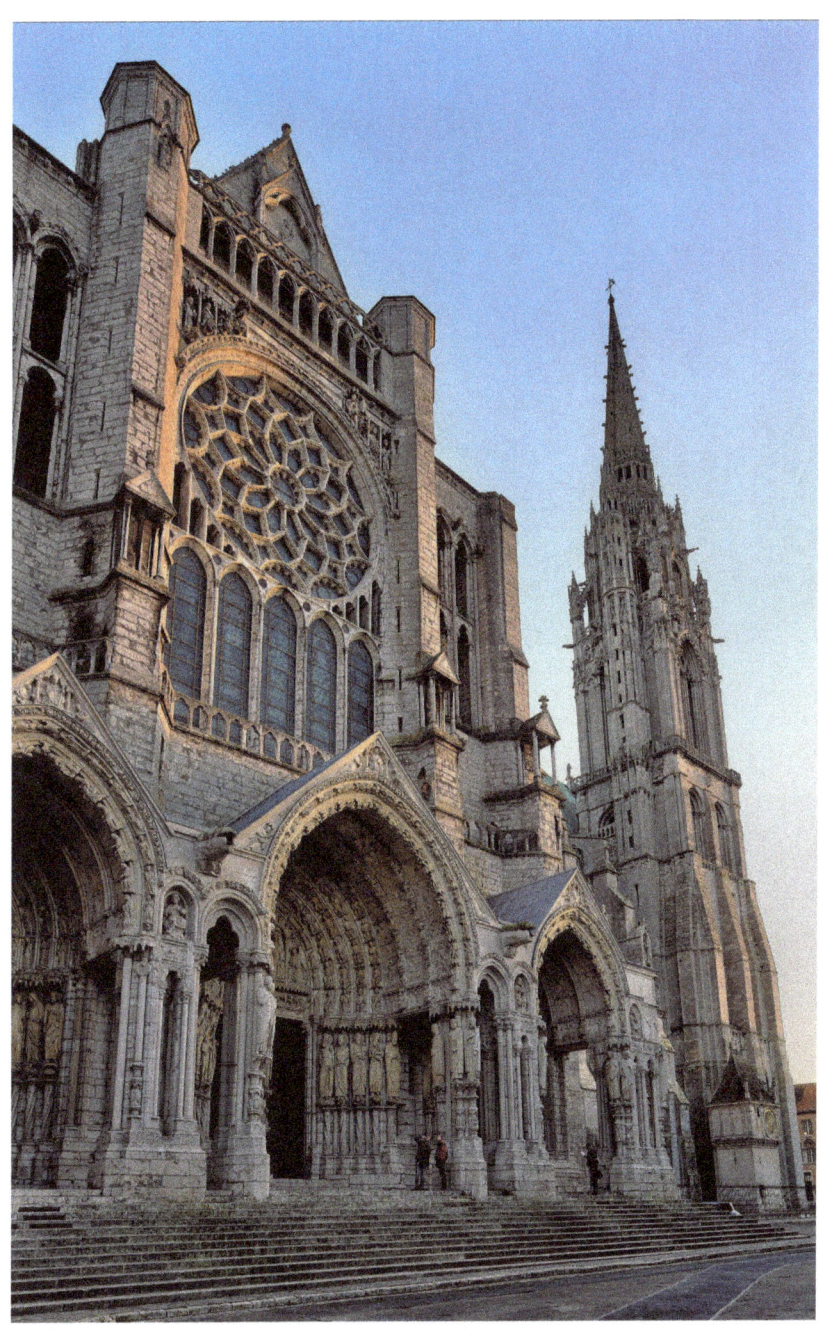

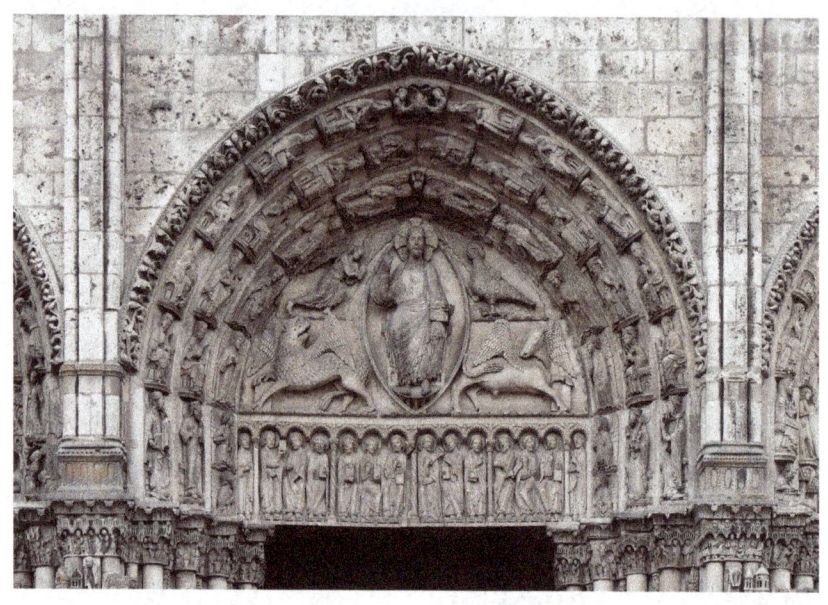

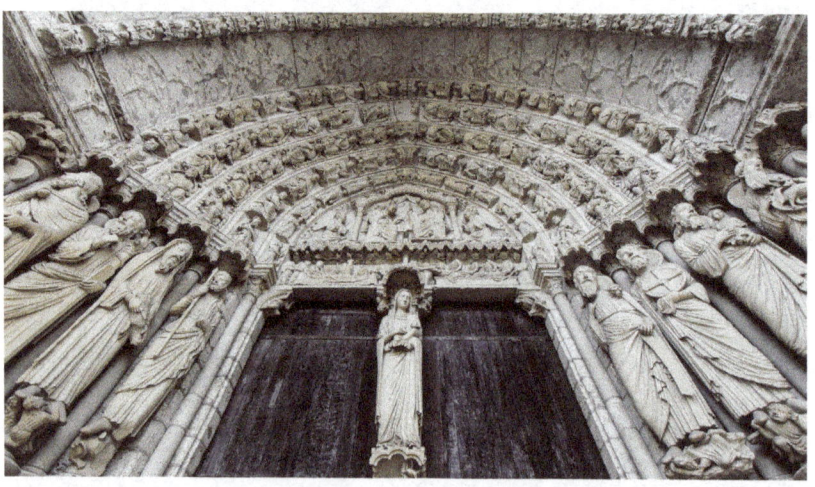

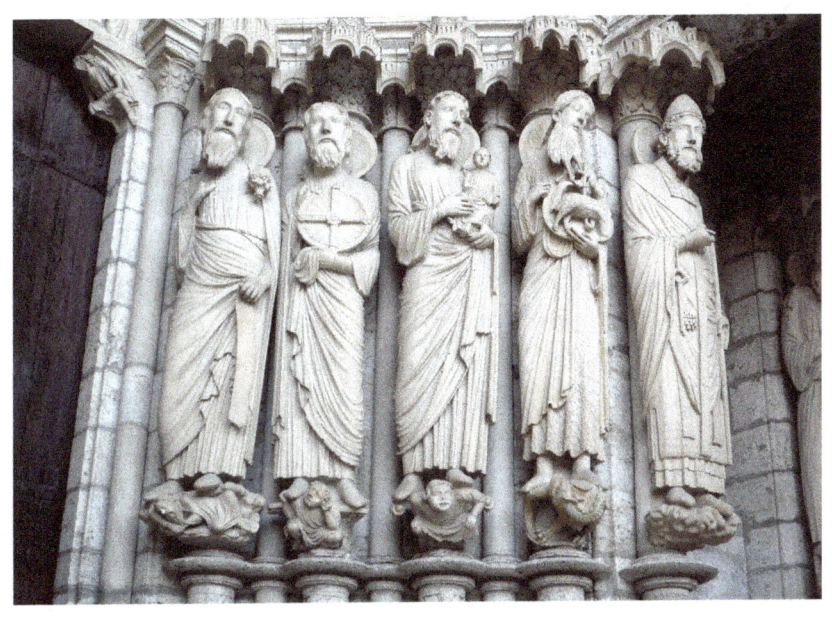

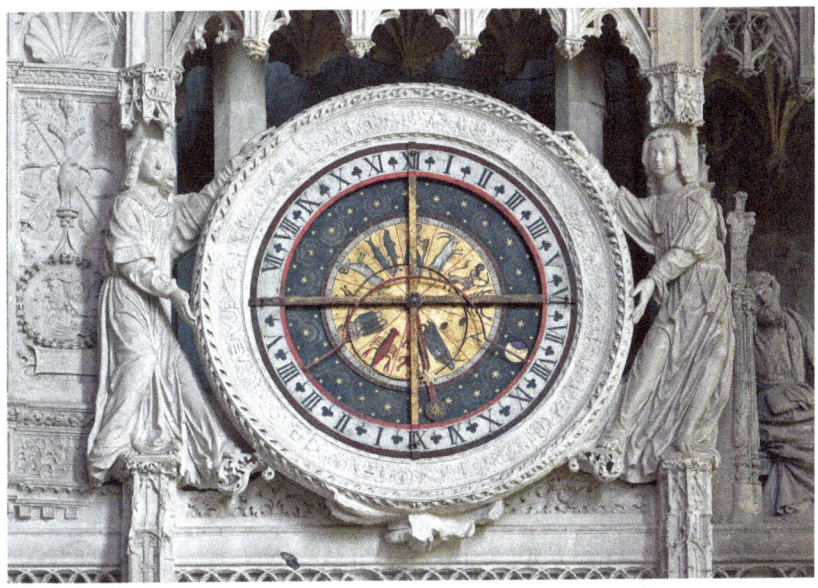

And so it goes for the thousands of statues that adorn the cathedral.

Now the ceremonies involved in worship participate in the same symbolism. In an admirable book to which I should like eventually to pay a full tribute, Émile Mâle analyzes the first part of the feast of Holy Saturday according to William Durandus's *Rationale of the Divine Offices*.

"Morning starts with all the lights being put out to indicate that the Old Law, which used to light up the world, is now abrogated.

"Then the celebrant blesses the new fire, a figure of the New Law. He brings it out of the flint to recall that Jesus Christ is, as Saint Paul says, the keystone of the world. At this point the bishop and the deacon make their way to the choir and stop before the Paschal candle."

William Durandus tells us that this candle is a threefold symbol. When it is unlit it symbolizes the dark pillar that guided the Hebrews by day, the Old Law, and the body of Jesus Christ. Once lit it signifies the pillar of light that Israel could see by night, the New Law, and the glorious body of the Risen Christ. The deacon alludes to this triple symbolism when he recites the *Exultet* before the candle.

But it is especially the resemblance between the candle and the Body of Jesus Christ that he emphasizes. He recalls that the spotless wax was produced by the bee, a creature both chaste and fruitful, like the Virgin who gave birth to the Savior. To bring out to the sense of sight the likeness of the wax to the divine body, he presses five grains of incense into the candle; these recall both the five wounds of Jesus Christ and the spices that the Holy Women had bought to embalm him. Lastly, he lights the candle with the new fire and all lamps throughout the church are lit to represent the New Law in the world.

Someone will say: "But all this is only an exceptional feast." Here is the interpretation of a daily ceremony: the Mass. You will see that it is no less symbolic.

"The deep and sorrowful chant of the *Introit* opens the ceremony: it proclaims the expectation of the patriarchs and prophets.

The clergy are in choir, the choir of the saints of the Old Law who yearn for the coming of the Messias and do not see Him. Then the bishop enters and appears as the living image of Jesus Christ. His arrival symbolizes the Advent of the Lord that the nations await. On great feast days, seven torches are born before him to recall that, as the prophet says, the seven gifts of the Holy Ghost rest upon the head of the Son of God. He processes under a triumphant canopy whose four bearers may be likened to the four Evangelists. Two acolytes walk to the right and left of this and represent Moses and Elias, who appeared at Mount Tabor on either side of Christ. They teach that Jesus held the authority of the Law and of the Prophets.

"The bishop sits on his throne and remains silent. He seems to take no part in the first part of the ceremony. His behavior contains a teaching: his silence recalls that the first years of the life of Christ were unknown and recollected. Meanwhile the subdeacon reaches the pulpit and reads the Epistle aloud towards the right. Here we catch a glimpse of the first act in the drama of our Redemption.

"This reading of the Epistle is the preaching of Saint John the Baptist in the desert. He speaks before the Saviour has begun to make Himself heard, but he speaks only to the Jews. For this reason, the subdeacon, an image of the Precursor, turns to the North, the direction of the Old Law. Once the lesson is read, he bows before the bishop, just as the Precursor bowed before Jesus Christ.

"The chanting of the Gradual follows the reading of the Epistle. It, too, refers to the mission of Saint John the Baptist: it symbolizes the exhortation to penance he directed towards the Jews on the eve of the new era.

"At last, the celebrant reads the Gospel. This is a solemn moment, for this is where the Messias's active life begins: for the first time, His voice is heard in the world. The reading of the Gospel is the very figure of his preaching.

"The creed follows the Gospel, just as the faith follows the proclamation of the truth. The twelve articles in the creed refer to the call of the Apostles.

"The very clothing the priest wears to the altar" and the objects used in worship amount to so many symbols, M. Mâle adds. "The chasuble, worn on top of the other garments, is charity, which is above all the commandments of the Law and is itself the supreme law. The stole, which the priest puts over his neck, is the light yoke of the Lord, and since it is written that every Christian must cherish this yoke, the priest kisses this yoke when he puts it on or takes it off. The bishop's two-pointed miter symbolizes the knowledge he must have of each of the Testaments; two ribbons are attached to it to recall that Holy Scripture is to be interpreted both literally and spiritually. The bell is the voice of the preachers and the timber from which it hangs is a figure of the Cross. Its rope, woven from three twisted threads, points to the threefold understanding of Scripture, which must be interpreted according to the threefold sense, i.e., historically, allegorically, and morally. When one takes the rope in hand to set the bell ringing, one symbolically expresses the fundamental truth that the knowledge of Scripture must lead to acts."

And in this way everything down to the least of the priest's gestures, down to the stole he wears, comes together to symbolize Him with the deep sentiment that gives life to the whole cathedral and which is, as M. Mâle puts it so well, the very genius of the Middle Ages.

Never has a sight comparable to such a giant mirror of knowledge, of the soul, and of history been presented to man's eyes and understanding. The same symbolism clutters even the music heard in the immense vessel. Its seven Gregorian tones are the figure of the seven virtues and the seven ages of the world. One may well say that a production of Wagner at Bayreuth does not amount to much next to the celebration of High Mass at the Chartres cathedral.

Doubtless only those who have studied the religious art of the Middle Ages are fully able to analyze the beauty of such a spectacle. That alone would justify the State's obligation to see to its preservation. This is precisely how the State underwrites the lectures at the *Collège de France*, even though they are intended only for a small number of people and, if compared to the total resurrection of a Solemn Mass in a Cathedral, seem like cold dissections; compared to the performance of such symphonies, the productions of our equally subsidized theaters answer to quite paltry literary demands. But let us hasten to add that the people who can read medieval symbolism fluently are not the only ones for whom the living cathedral, that is to say the sculpted, painted, singing cathedral is the greatest of spectacles, as one can feel music without knowing [the science of] harmony. I am well aware that Ruskin, when he was demonstrating what spiritual reasons explain the arrangement of chapels in cathedral apses, declared: "Never will you be able to delight in architectural forms unless you are in sympathy with the thinking from which they arose." Still, we all know the ignorant man, the simple dreamer, who walks into a cathedral without any effort at understanding yet is overwhelmed by his emotions and receives an impression which, though perhaps less precise, is certainly just as strong. As a literary witness to this state of mind, admittedly quite different from that of the learned person of whom we were speaking a moment ago and who walks in a cathedral "as in a forest of symbols that gaze on him with familiar glances," yet which allows for a vague but powerful emotion in a cathedral during the liturgy, I shall quote Renan's beautiful text *The Double Prayer*:

> One of the most beautiful religious spectacles one can still contemplate today (and which one may soon no longer be able to contemplate, if the House of Representatives passes the Briand bill) is that which the ancient cathedral of Quimper presents at dusk. Once darkness has filled the vast building's side aisles, the faithful of both sexes gather in the nave and sing evensong in the Breton language with a simple and moving rhythm. The cathedral is lit only by two or three lamps. In the nave, the men are on one side, standing; on the other side, the kneeling women form a motionless sea of white headdresses. The two halves sing in alternation, and the phrase that one of the choirs begins is finished by the

other. What they sing is quite beautiful. As I heard it, I felt that with a few changes it might be fitted to every state of humanity. Above all it made me dream of a prayer which, with a few variations, might suit men and women equally.

There are many gradations between this reverie, which is not without its charm, and the religious art "connoisseur's" more conscious joys. Let us firmly keep in mind the case of Gustave Flaubert, who studied—albeit with a view to interpreting it within a modern outlook—one of the most beautiful parts of the Catholic liturgy:

> The priest dipped his thumb in the holy oil and began to anoint her eyes first . . . then her nostrils, so fond of warm breezes and of the scents of love, her hands that had found their delight in sweet caresses . . . lastly her feet, which had been so swift in running to satisfy her desires, and which now would walk no more.

There is therefore more than one way of dreaming before this artistic accomplishment—the most complete ever, since all of the arts collaborated in it—of the greatest dream to which humanity ever rose; this mansion is grand enough for us all to find our place in it. The cathedral, which shelters so many saints, patriarchs, prophets, apostles, kings, confessors, and martyrs that whole generations huddle in supplication and anxiety all the way to the porch entrances and, trembling, raise the edifice as a long groan under heaven while the angels smilingly lean over from the top of the galleries which, in the evening's blue and rose incense and the morning's blinding gold, do seem to be "heaven's balconies"—the cathedral, in its vastness, can grant asylum both to the man of letters and to the man of faith, to the vague dreamer as well as to the archeologist. All that matters is that it remains alive and that France should not find herself transformed overnight into a dried-up shore on which giant chiseled shells seem marooned, emptied of the life that once lived in them, and no longer able even to give to an ear leaning in on them a distant rumor from long ago—mere museum pieces and icy museums themselves. "It is not too late," André Hallays wrote some years ago, to bring up a gruesome idea which, they say, was hatched in the brains of a few citizens of Vézelay. They wanted the church of Vézelay to be decommissioned. Such is the silliness that anticlericalism inspires. Decommissioning that basilica amounts to taking away what little soul it has left. Once the little lamp that shines deep in the sanctuary has been snuffed out, Vézelay will become no more than an archeological curiosity. The tomb-like odor of museums is all that will give breath in it.

Things keep their beauty and their life only by continuously carrying out the task for which they were intended, even if they should slowly die at it. Does anyone believe that, in museums of comparative sculpture, the plaster casts of the famous sculpted wooden choir stalls of the Cathedral of Amiens can give an idea of the stalls themselves in their august yet still functional antiquity? Whereas a museum guard keeps us from getting too close to their plaster casts, the pricelessly precious stalls, which are so old, so illustrious, and so beautiful, continue to carry out their humble task in the cathedral of Amiens—which they have been doing for centuries to the great satisfaction of the citizens of Amiens—just as those artists who, while having become famous, yet still keep up a small job or give lessons. This task consists in bearing bodies even before they instruct souls, and that is what, folded down and showing their upper side, they humbly do during the offices. More than this: the perpetually worn wood of these stalls has slowly acquired, or rather let seep through, that dark purple that is as it were its heart and which the eye that has once fallen prey to its charm prefers to everything else, to the point of being unable even to look at the colors of the paintings which, after this, seem rough and plain. Then one experiences something like ebriety as one savors, in the wood's ever more blazing ardor, what is so to speak the tree's sap overflowing in time. The naïve figures sculpted in it receive something like a twofold nature from the material in which they live. And generations have variously polished all of these Amiens-born fruits, flowers, leaves, and vegetation that the Amiens sculptor sculpted in Amiens wood, thus bringing out those wonderful contrasting tones in which the differently-colored leaf stands out from the twig; this brings to mind the noble accents that M. Gallé has been able to draw out of the oak's harmonious heart.

The cathedral, if M. Briand's bill were passed, would find itself closed and unable to provide the Mass and prayers not just for the canons who perform the services in those stalls whose armrests, misericords, and banister tell of the Old and New Testaments, nor only for the people filling up the immense nave. We were just saying that nearly every image in a cathedral is a symbol. Yet some are not. Such are the painted or sculpted pictures of those who, having contributed their pennies to the decoration of the cathedral, wished to keep a place in it forever, so that they might silently follow the services and noiselessly participate in prayer from a niche's balustrade or the recess of a stained-glass window, *in saecula saeculorum*. We know that since the oxen of Laon had christianly drawn the construction materials for the cathedral up the hill from which it rises, the architect rewarded them by setting up their statues at the feet of the towers. You can see them to this day as, in the din of the bells and the pooling sunlight, they raise their horned heads above the colossal holy arch towards the horizon of the French plains—their "inner dream." That was the best that could be done for beasts: for men, better was granted.

They went into the church. There they took their place, which would be theirs after death and from which, just as during their lifetime, they could go on following the divine sacrifice. In some cases, leaning out of their marble tomb, they turn their heads slightly to the Gospel or to the Epistle side and can glimpse and feel around them, as they can in Brou, the tight and tireless interlacing of crest flowers and initials; sometimes, as in Dijon, they keep the bright colors of life even in their tombs. In other cases, from the recess of a stained-glass window, in their crimson, ultramarine, or azure cloaks catching the sun and blazing up with it, they fill its transparent rays with color and suddenly let them loose, multicolored and aimlessly wandering about the nave, tingeing it with their wild and lazy splendor, with their palpable unreality. In this way they remain donors, who, for this very reason, have deserved perpetual prayers. And all of them want the Holy Ghost, when He will come down from the Church, really to recognize His own. It is not just the queen and the princes who wear their insignia, their crown, or their collar of the Golden Fleece: money changers are portrayed proving the title of coins; furriers sell their furs (see Mâle for reproductions of those windows); butchers slaughter cows; knights wear their coats of arms; sculptors cut capitals. Oh! all of you in your stained-glass windows in Chartres, in Tours, in Bourges, in Sens, in Auxerre, in Troyes, in Clermont-Ferrand, in Toulouse, ye coopers, furriers, grocers, pilgrims, laborers, armorers, weavers, stonemasons, butchers, basket weavers, cobblers, money changers, O ye, great silent democracy, ye faithful obstinately wanting to hear the Office, who are not dematerialized but more beautiful than in your living days now in the glory of heaven and the blood that is your precious glass: no longer will you hear the Mass you had guaranteed for yourselves by donating the best part of your pennies to building this church. As the profound saying goes, the dead no longer govern the living. And the forgetful living stop fulfilling the wishes of the dead.

But let the ruby coopers and the rose and silver basket weavers inscribe the backdrop of their stained glass with the "silent protest" that M. Jaurès could so eloquently give us and which we beg him to bring to the ears of the representatives. Leaving aside that innumerable and silent people, the ancestors of the electors for whom the House has such little concern, let us at last summarize:

First: safeguarding the most beautiful works of French architecture and sculpture, which *will die* on the day that they no longer serve the worship for which they were born, which is their function just as they are its organs, which explains them because it is their soul, makes it the government's duty to demand that worship be offered in the cathedrals in perpetuity, while the Briand bill authorizes it to turn the cathedrals into whatever museums or conference halls (in the best of cases) it pleases after a few years, and even if the government does not undertake to do so, it authorizes the clergy (and, since it will no longer be subsidized, compels it) no longer to celebrate the offices in them if it finds the rent too high.

Second: the preservation of the greatest historic yet living artistic production imaginable, for the reconstruction of which, if it did not already exist, no one would shrink from spending millions, namely the cathedral Mass, makes it the government's duty to subsidize the Catholic Church for the upkeep of a worship that is far more relevant to the conservation of the noblest French art (to continue our strictly worldly perspective) than the conservatories, theaters, concert-halls, ancient tragedy reconstitutions at the theater of Orange, etc. etc., all of which enterprises have questionable artistic aims and maintain lackluster productions (how do *Le Jour*, *L'Aventurière*, or *Le Gendre de M. Poirier* stand up to the choir of Beauvais or the statues of Rheims?), whereas the masterpiece that is the medieval cathedral, with its thousands of painted or sculpted figures, its chants, its services, is the noblest of all the works to which the genius of France has ever risen.

And so far in this article we have mentioned only the cathedrals, in order to present the consequences of the Briand bill in their most striking form, the form most apt to shock the reader's mind. But obviously this distinction between cathedral churches and others is quite artificial, since it sufficed, on a feast day, to erect the bishop's *cathedra* in a church to turn it into a cathedral for a day. What I have said about the cathedrals applies to all the beautiful churches of France, and it is a matter of common knowledge that there are thousands of them. On the French road so beautiful among sainfoin fields and apple orchards lining up on either side to let it through, with nearly every step you will see a steeple rising against stormy or peaceful horizons. On mixed days of rain and sun, it is set across a rainbow which, as a mystical halo reflected in the nearby heaven within the half-open church, juxtaposes its rich and distinct stained-glass colors on the sky. With nearly every step you see a steeple rising above the earth-gazing houses as an ideal, soaring amid the bell's voices with which, if you come near, the birds' song mingles. Well: you may often positively state that the church above which it rises contains beautiful and grave sculpted and painted thoughts, as well as other thoughts which, since they are not called to the same distinct life, have remained vaguer, in a state of beautiful architectural lines that are more obscure yet also more powerful, as well as able to carry our imagination away in their upward flight or to enclose it entirely within the curve of their pitch. There, from a Romanesque balcony's charming banisters, or from the mysterious threshold of a half-open Gothic porch sleeping in the shade of the grand trees all around that marries the sun to the church's illumined obscurity within, we must go on to see the procession coming out of the multicolored shade falling from the stone trees of the nave and follow, as in the countryside among the squat pillars and their flowery and fruited capitals, those paths regarding which one may say, as the prophet said of the Lord: "All of his paths are peace."[4]

Finally, we have only mentioned an artistic interest in all of this. This is not to say that the Briand bill does not threaten other interests, or that we are indifferent to them. This, however, is the point of view we wanted to take. The clergy would be mistaken if it turned away support from artists. For when one sees how many representatives, once they have finished passing anticlerical laws, go off on a tour of the cathedrals of England, of France, or of Italy, bring back an old chasuble for their wife to turn into a coat or a door-curtain, draw up secularization plans in offices where hangs a photographed version of the Entombment, haggle over an altarpiece volet with an antique dealer, go out into the countryside to fetch church stall fragments to serve as umbrella stands in their parlors, and, on Good Friday, "religiously," as they say, listen to the *Missa Papae Marcelli* at the "Schola Cantorum" if not at Sainte-Geneviève, one may think that once we persuade all persons of good taste of the government's duty to subsidize worship, we shall have found allies, and raised against the Briand bill any number of representatives, even anticlerical ones.

---

4. Cf. Proverbs 3:17, speaking of Wisdom: "Her ways are beautiful ways, and all her paths are peaceable."

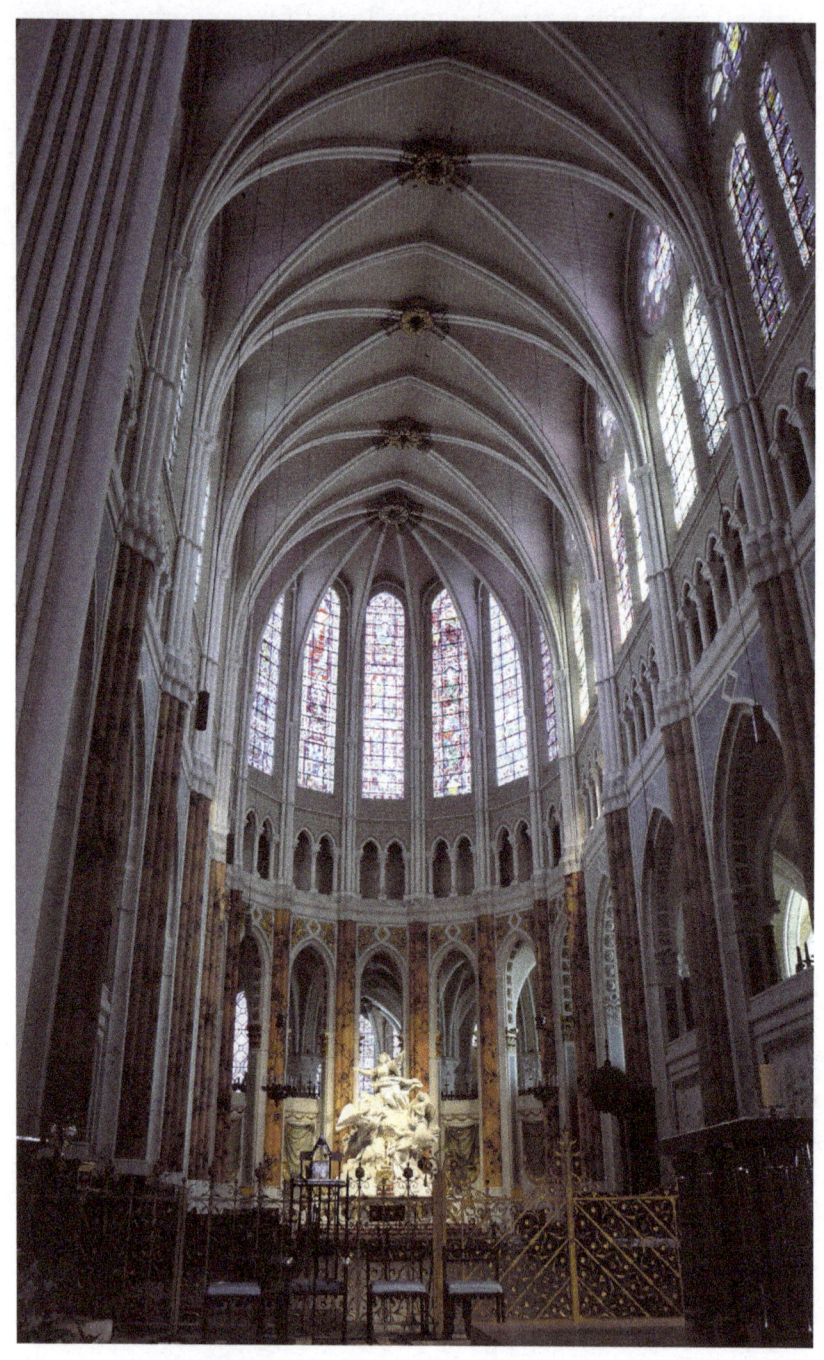

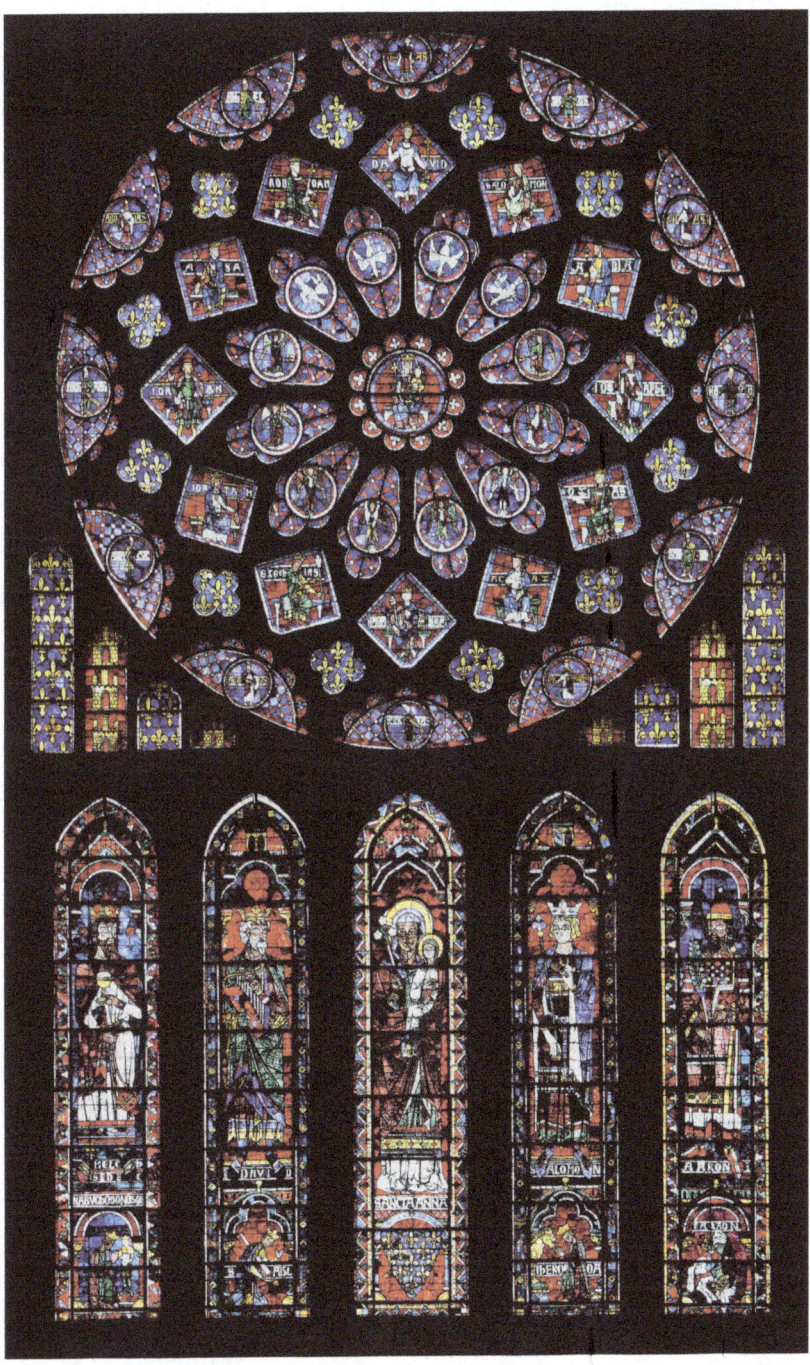

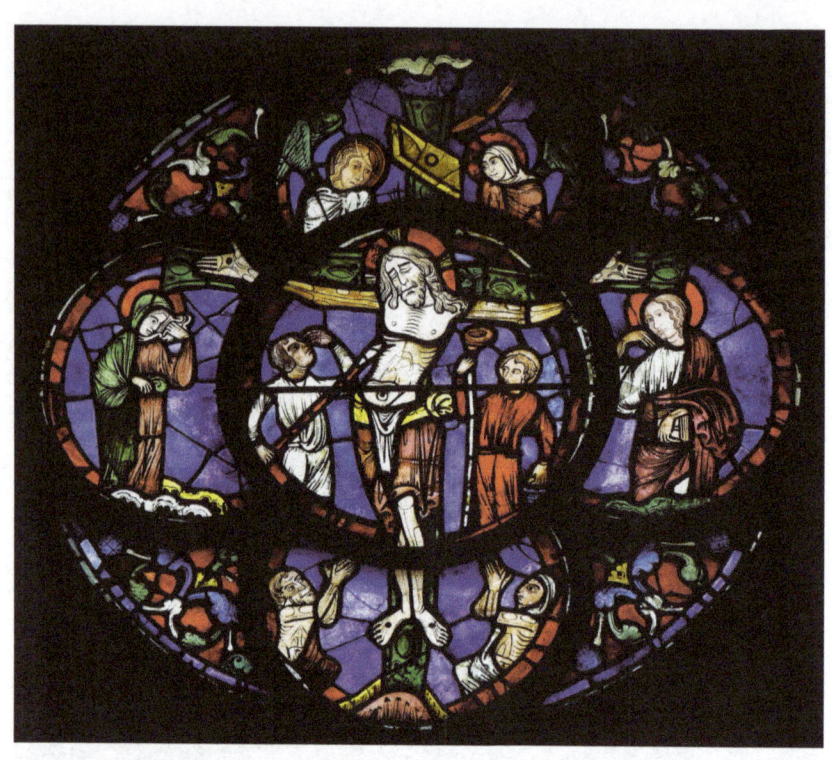

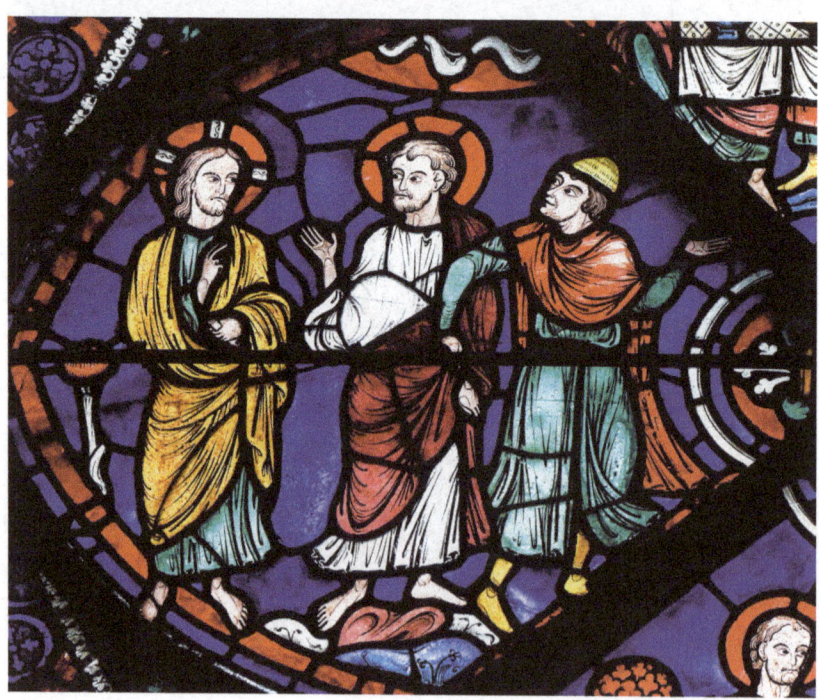

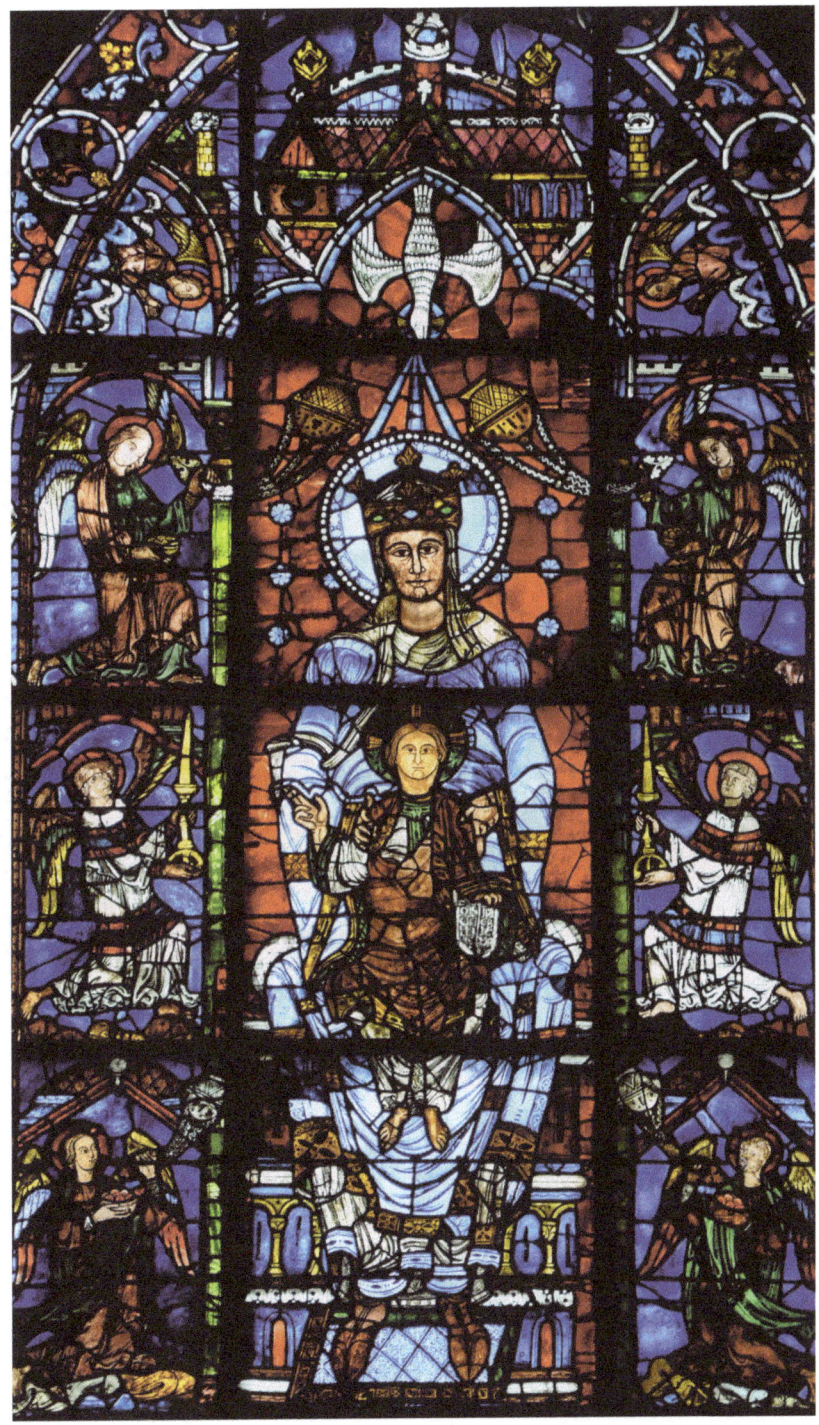

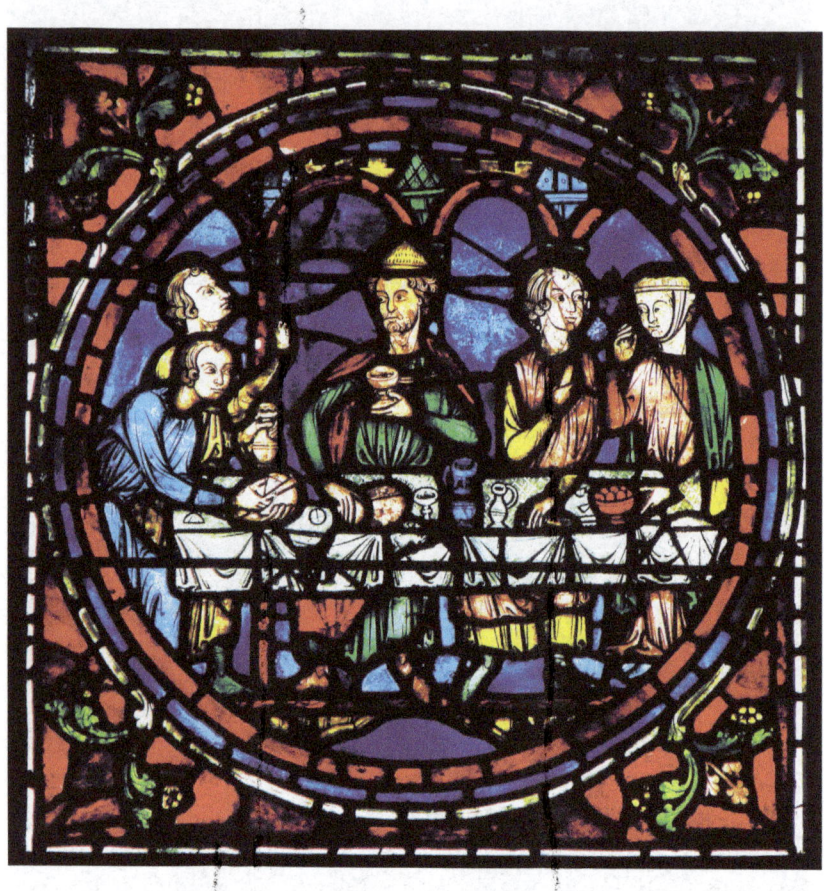

AFTERWORD

Will Life Return to Cathedrals?

When I was in high school and college, I wrote a good deal of poetry. It started off free-form, in that lazy way moderns have, but soon, under the influence of Gerard Manley Hopkins, Francis Thompson, T.S. Eliot, and like representatives of "The *Other* Modern," I began to try my hand at more traditional forms. The high point was a one-act play, written in heroic couplets, about the destruction of a monastery by French revolutionaries, written at Georgetown University in the fall of 1989, a bicentennial opportunity that could not be missed, at a location that was gorging on the revolution's fruits. Then, in a sort of puritanical phase, I destroyed all of this verse—a foolish act I now regret. But one poem somehow escaped the purge. It's not my best, but it has sentimental value . . . and it is relevant to my story.

> Church light-filled! stretto-spires heavenward flying
>   To greet God, Maker, Master, Harmony
> Of souls; Church truth-belov'd, deceit-denying,
>   Inflamed with amorous divinity:
> O mighty Chartres (in glass a thousand tales
>   Beyond world's ends), stone bends to supplicate
> The faithful Virgin, whom our prayer assails
>   Meek, confident. "I bid thee, hurl this weight
> Of sin into the sea, a mountain planted
>   Deep." Thus the villager; thus lord and king,
> All men, athirst for light, contritely panted,
>   Pilgrims laved and fed at grace's spring.
>   O Virgin, glass-beheld, in sculpture fair,
>   I beg thee: Hear with living ears my prayer.

I wrote this poem in high school not because I had already been to Chartres cathedral or had immediate prospects of visiting, but because I had just finished reading Henry Adams's *Mont Saint Michel and Chartres*, in which a cultivated agnostic enthuses over medieval Catholic France. I was inspired, too, just by his telling of the travelogue, by his array of impressions.

The year in which Henry Adams privately published *Mont Saint Michel and Chartres*—1904—happens to have been the same year in which the French liberal unbeliever, Marcel Proust, published the newspaper article contained in this volume. The similarities are remarkable: two introspective intellectuals, cultured agnostics on opposite shores, who were fascinated by the glories of Gothic art and architecture ("the masterpiece that is the medieval cathedral, with its thousands of painted or sculpted figures, its chants, its services, is the noblest of all the works to which the genius of France has ever risen," writes Proust)—cultural relics of what was, to them, a superannuated religion, yet a religion whose relics, transmitted down through the ages, still touched and healed their fellow men in the present time. Surely Proust and Adams must have had analogous experiences in order to write as movingly as they did of the incomparable value of the French churches born of divine faith. Proust in particular saw, or rather felt, that the edifices built for this sublime *cultus* cried out to be worshiped in, for that was their soul, their source of life: "The most beautiful works of French architecture and sculpture . . . *will die* on the day that they no longer serve the worship for which they were born, which is their function just as they are its organs, which explains them because it is their soul."

The most famous chapter in Adams's book is entitled "The Virgin and the Dynamo": a contrast between the Queen of Heaven whose devotees at Chartres built her a marvelous shrine full of radiance, and the impersonal forty-foot electrical generator that Adams had beheld at the Great Exposition in Paris in 1900, symbol of a mechanistic, industrialized civilization. This contrast—whether cast in terms of Adams's competition between a virgin mother's shrine and a lifeless generator, or in Proust's more subtle opposition between the effete aestheticism of Bayreuth or scholarly reconstructions of ancient tragedies and the living Christian faith that sustained the rites still celebrated in the places built to house them[5]—invites us to consider the two aspects from which technology can be evaluated: quantitative and qualitative. Quantitative superiority means, for example, being able to lift a larger number of heavier objects faster, or being able to produce more books more quickly. Qualitative superiority means being able to craft a beautiful object such as a statue, a stained-glass window, or an illuminated manuscript, even if it takes a very long time and the objects are comparatively few in number. This distinction having been made, it is easy to draw the conclusion that medieval technology was superior to modern in a *qualitative* sense, while modern technology is superior to medieval only in a quantitative sense. In the end, which is the more important of the two?

"In the modern world of measurements," writes André Gushurst-Moore, "success is defined in physical terms, by that which is faster, bigger, taller—the celebration of power."[6] One is reminded of the difference between the ancient Roman lectionary still contained in the Tridentine missal, as perfectly suited for its purpose as a slender Gothic column or a vaulted arch, and the modern multi-volume lectionary used for the Novus Ordo, a heaped-up pile of Soviet-style apartment blocs.

---

5. Remember, this is 1904: Pope Pius X, reigning on the Chair of St. Peter, had released one year before the motu proprio *Tra le Sollecitudini* restoring Gregorian chant to its pride of place. The "medieval" worship of the Church was alive and (at least in some places) well, with excellent prospects for the future. Dom Guéranger's pioneering work in promoting solemn monastic liturgy was bearing fruit in the healthy phase of the Liturgical Movement, intent on spreading knowledge and love of the Church's bimillennial heritage.

6. *Glory in All Things: St. Benedict and Catholic Education Today* (Brooklyn: Angelico Press, 2019), 14.

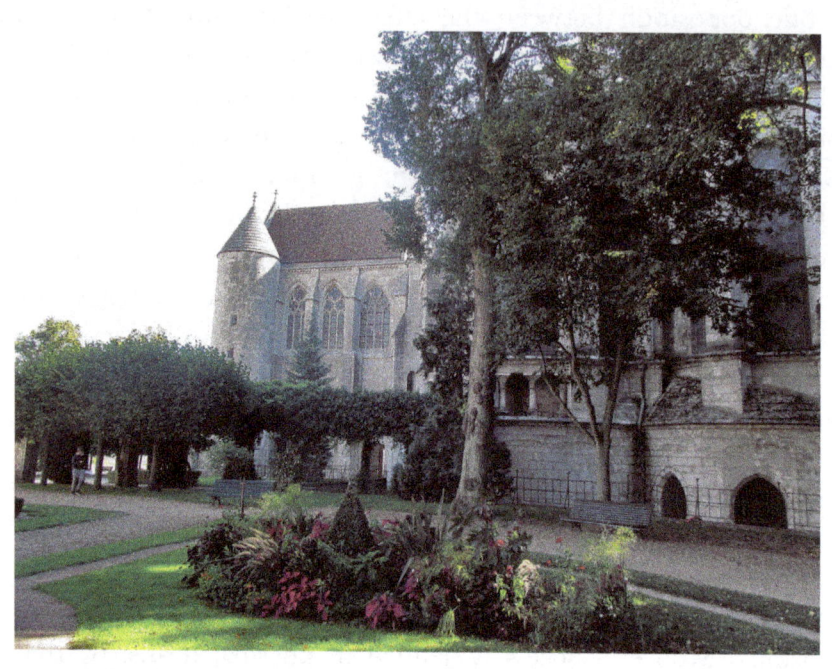

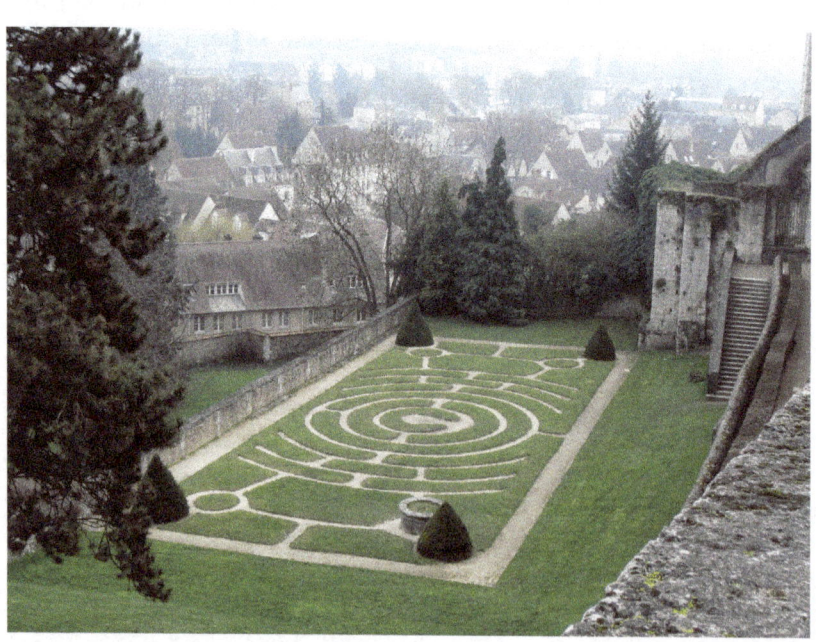

***

In 2015, about twenty-five years after writing that poem, I finally made it to Chartres. I was not among those jolly, flag-bearing strong souls who make the trek by foot singing through mud and rain on the famous pilgrimage from Paris to Chartres—one might say, from the Dynamo to the Virgin. The grace of this visitation came rather during a father-son trip made while I was on sabbatical.

My son and I arrived at the sleepy medieval town on a train from Paris. Given our limited time, we had had to make a difficult choice: visit St. Denis, the first of Gothic churches, or Chartres, the finest of them. St. Thérèse's "I choose all!" strategy was not going to work in this situation. We agreed on Chartres, the very name of which is like sweet mead or glistening water.

When I first caught sight of the spires, my heart began to race. As we drew near, I fell in love with her face, which I knew was no mere facade but an earnest of the vastitude within, as in the verse *omnis gloria eius filiae regis ab intus* (Psalm 44:14).[7] And when we entered, and my eyes had adjusted to the soothing half-light, I was transported out of myself and did not return to my shoes for a long time: my mind was soaring elsewhere, my eyes lost in dizzying vaults and shimmering glass. I do not know how to describe my feelings, except to say with Dionysius the Areopagite: it was no mere learning of divine things, but a suffering of them.

***

After we had left, I wrote the following in my journal.

"October 1. Chartres Cathedral is, indeed, a 'miracle in stone and glass.' I have never seen a church more beautiful than this. Nothing in Rome can even begin to compare with it. It utterly

---

7. Psalm 44:14–15: "All the glory of the king's daughter is within in golden borders, clothed round about with varieties."

lacks the pomposity, worldliness, self-importance, and humanistic vanity of the Renaissance structures of Italy, the self-conscious triumphalism of the Counter-Reformation Baroque. It is grand but always turned heavenwards—and turning one's soul heavenwards. There is deep humility and prayer built into, nay fused with, this immensely impressive edifice. Everywhere God is glorified in His saints, in the light that pours through the windows, ever shifting as the day proceeds, in the colors, the eyes, the sculptures . . . I said to J.: it is nothing less than the Bible in glass and stone. To say that medievals who could understand these images were 'illiterates' would be to say that moderns who cannot are idiots.

"Baroque art stresses God become man, heaven penetrating into this world—in the sacraments, the Eucharist, the priesthood, the Church *visible* as a body. It is deliberately sensual, bodily, plastic, dramatic. Gothic speaks rather of man aspiring to God, earth being lifted up to heaven, the ascent of the soul via Christ to God. It is straining to leave the body, to let the light suffuse and transfigure everything visible so that it might shine with intimations of divinity and immortality. The light-colored stone works together with the great height and the exquisite windows to create an effect of weightless uplift: *Sursum corda*. It is not so much dramatic as symbolic—more prayer than propaganda. It delivers its message with the existential shock of beauty. But how many are receptive to this shock anymore? Sure, every visitor can say: 'It's lovely' or 'it's amazing,' but does it have a deep and lasting impact on them? In these times, when everyone's eyes are glued to smartphones, when their ears are stuffed with earbuds, the words of Jesus take on a pitiful sound: 'He who has ears to hear, let him hear; he who has eyes to see, let him see.'[8]

"Nothing we have done in architecture could even compare with Chartres, let alone equal it or surpass it. Built by people with so little technology compared to ours! But they had faith, vision,

---

8. Proust was more optimistic in his day: "Still, we all know the ignorant man, the simple dreamer, who walks into a cathedral without any effort at understanding yet is overwhelmed by his emotions and receives an impression which, though perhaps less precise, is certainly just as strong."

wonder, ambition, and the desire to give God the greatest and best. Yet moderns are arrogant, and put down the Middle Ages. This shows how blind we really are (or have become).

"October 2. Low Mass [at Église Saint-Eugène-Sainte-Cécile in Paris] for the feast of the Guardian Angels was beautiful—so comforting to have the same Mass, the true Mass, the only real Mass of the Catholic Church—the same everywhere in the world. J. said: 'Let's light a candle for the restoration of tradition.' So we lit two candles, at a side altar of St. Anthony. My prayer was: 'Lord, may the Church's youth be renewed like the eagle's.'"

* * *

The visit to Chartres changed my life. I was reduced to dust before a theophany of absolute meaning. With a colossal immediacy and certitude, I apprehended the truth, in a way both intuitive and visceral, that high medieval Catholic culture was not merely one among many flowerings of the Christian Faith; it was the quintessential epiphany of what John Henry Newman called the "Idea" of Christianity. It was its preeminent cultural embodiment, exhibiting a sublime conformity of thought and thing, ideal and incarnation, belief and building, aspiration and aesthetic, the likes of which the world had never seen before and has never seen since.

Chartres Cathedral was finished eight hundred years ago, in 1220, four years before the birth of St. Thomas Aquinas in Roccasecca, and six years before the death of St. Francis in Assisi. It came from the age that gave us the most radical imitator of Christ and first stigmatist, who unleashed a revolution very different from feverish dreams of *liberté, égalité, fraternité*. It came from the era that gave us the greatest theologian of the Western Church, the Angelic Doctor, still the exemplary teacher and disciple of the harmony of faith and reason. Jacques Maritain wrote: "Our Lady of Chartres is as much a marvel of logic as the *Summa* of St. Thomas."[9]

---

9. *Art and Scholasticism* (Providence, RI: Cluny Media, 2020), 50.

I had already been a traditionalist and an integralist for many years—theoretically. The experience of the cathedral shattered in me the last psychological outposts of nominalism, rationalism, liberalism, and every other -ism of mirthless modernity. I could see, hear, smell, taste, and touch the glory of Christendom—even at a distance of so many centuries. It was a consoling sight, an invigorating melody, a captivating smell, a foretaste of heaven, a touch that wounded as it healed. It roused awake the *sensus fidei*, the *sensus catholicus* in my soul. Somehow—I think for the first time—I had an overwhelming sense of the humble glory of *being Catholic*.

The experience was a turning point, too, in my thinking about the liturgy. Prior to this, I had been willing to entertain the so-called "reform of the reform" as a possibility; I played my part in adding "smells and bells" to the modern papal rite of Paul VI. Afterwards, I felt it was nothing but vanity and vexation of spirit, as if one had been asked to reconstruct Chartres with Lego bricks.

Visiting the cathedral with me that first day of October, my adolescent son was similarly overwhelmed. He said: "If I tried to describe this place to someone who had never been here, he wouldn't believe me. He would think I was exaggerating, making stuff up. And then . . . you wouldn't actually be able to find the right words anyway."[10]

Isn't this the experience so many of us have with the traditional Latin Mass when we try to talk about it with others, when we try to get them interested in *their own* birthright—in the words of Fr. Faber, "the most beautiful thing this side of heaven," or, in

---

10. At the time, neither of us knew about Joris-Karl Huysmans's novel *The Cathedral*, written in 1898, in which the autobiographical protagonist Durtal explores the cathedral of Chartres and describes it in luxurious detail. One might see a lesson for the twenty-first century in this nineteenth-century former decadent (*Against Nature*) and sometime-dabbler in Satanism (*The Damned*) who was drawn into the Church by the Catholicism of his day, with its vital link to the Middle Ages (*En Route, The Cathedral, The Oblate*). Should anyone be surprised that youths today are attracted not by a manufactured up-to-date liturgy of the sixties and seventies, but by the restored traditional rites of the Church—the same ones Proust and Huysmans would have seen and heard?

Proust's words, "the greatest historic yet living artistic production imaginable"?

Once a year, thanks to the Chartres pilgrimage, this silent, patient house of God resounds again in melodious chant, as the great Roman Pontifical Mass is celebrated at the high altar—that liturgy for which this building and thousands of others of similar ambition were built, and without which they seem absurdly overdone: gigantic relics we no longer know how to venerate, embarrassments in a world of comfort, efficiency, and sensible mediocrity. Our chronic inferiority, our fumbling incapacity in the face of earnest faith and grandeur of soul, extends beyond architecture to the sacred music meant to fill it with angelic euphony. According to the most recent ecumenical council, "the musical tradition of the universal Church is a treasure of inestimable value, greater even than that of any other art"[11]—an astonishing claim to think about when you are standing in front of or inside of Chartres cathedral. The reason given? This music, above all Gregorian chant, *is* the sacred liturgy—bone and flesh of it, in a way that no building could ever be. Yet that means the music stands or falls with the liturgical rite.[12] If the rite and its music are perfectly conformed to each other, they create a sonic temple that harmonizes with the visual temple. All the traditional art forms cohere in the liturgy that stands at their center. Proust, again, puts his finger on the truth: "One may well say that a production of Wagner at Bayreuth does not amount to much next to the celebration of High Mass at the Chartres cathedral." Today we can give this saying a melancholy twist: "One may well say that a Catholic Mass *à la mode* does not amount to much next to

---

11. *Sacrosanctum Concilium*, n. 112.

12. There was a mighty battle over the wording of *Sacrosanctum Concilium* Chapter VI, on sacred music. The principal drafter, Msgr. Johannes Overath, won the battle but lost the war: after the Council, this chapter was ignored by all who "implemented" the conciliar constitution, with Paul VI leading the way in his hand-wringing eulogy for Latin and Gregorian chant given in the form of a general audience on November 26, 1969, where he attempted to explain why his *Novus Ordo Missae* would dispense with them.

the production of any classic play or opera." If our author is right to say that "Catholic liturgy and the architecture and sculpture of our cathedrals form a whole, for they stem from the same symbolism," we will be justified in concluding that the only liturgy capable of bringing life back to the churches, great and small, is the one they were designed to shelter, and no other.

* * *

Chartres, this miracle of a cathedral, was almost destroyed with explosives at the time of the French Revolution, during the Reign of Terror (September 1793 to July 1794). It was spared, apparently, only when a local architect pointed out how much trouble it would be to clean up the vast amount of rubble. For many years it lay idle and vacant, one of countless "Temples of Reason" proclaimed by the Revolution, with no Holy Sacrifice offered on its altars.

A far more subtle though no less effective cancellation of its *raison d'être* occurred less than two centuries later when Paul VI made the liturgy itself into a temple of reason and extinguished the mystical flame of Catholic worship. To our everlasting shame, it was not radical Jacobins but surpliced churchmen who undertook the more barbaric work of destroying the traditional Mass that constitutes the single greatest work of art in the Christian West—greater, by far, even than the Gothic church architecture of France, or the heritage of Gregorian chant and polyphony, for it was nothing less than this *opus Dei* or "work of God" that inspired everything else surrounding it and coupled with it. A German author, Karl Lechner, observed:

Out of the Mass, among other things, the most profound splendor and ingenious fullness of the Catholic Church's architectural style has grown . . . Only on account of this worship can the proud majesty of a Gothic cathedral be understood . . . . But Romanesque architecture, too, has its necessary requirement in the service of the Mass . . . . Without the High Mass, no master builder of the spirited Middle Ages would have developed the basilica to this sublime, serious, and magnificent style. Without the Catholic service, neither Raphael nor Fra Angelico, Hubert van Eyck nor the younger Holbein, nor Lorenzo Ghiberti, Veit Stoss, and Peter Vischer would have brought to light the wonders of their brush and chisel, and adorned the Church of God on earth with a wealth of holy beauty that will remain a gem for all ages.[13]

The Mass of which Lechner wrote in 1877 was, of course, the Tridentine rite. The Novus Ordo could never have inspired Romanesque or Gothic architecture. This inspiration came from the Romano-Gallican liturgy of the Middle Ages, suffused with Carolingian "court ritual" and demanding a setting of gold and silver worthy of such a dazzling jewel.

The Liturgical Movement's cancer phase after World War II was driven by a number of principles, not all of them compatible with each other. Practically speaking, however, there was broad agreement about one thing: that which was medieval had, by and large, to be expunged. It lacked the supposed domesticity and familiarity of the early Church—so it was said; in reality this meant it did not accord with the sterile Cartesian ideals of simplicity and clarity inherited from the same Enlightenment rationalism that gave us the French Revolution. The liturgical reformers, like their precursors at the Synod of Pistoia (1786), and *their* precursors

---

13. K. Lechler, *Die Confessionen in ihrem Verhältnisse zu Christus* (Heilbronn: Verlag Gebr. Henninger, 1877), 166f., cited by Michael Fiedrowicz in *The Traditional Mass: History, Form, and Theology of the Classical Roman Rite*, trans. Rose Pfeifer (Brooklyn, NY: Angelico Press, 2020), 49, n17.

in the Protestant revolt, viewed the medieval period as an age of extravagant superstition, speculation without scholarship, fanciful mysticism, remote otherworldliness. In the name of Modernity and its Progress, medieval liturgy, medieval chant and architecture and theology (scholasticism) had to be purged from the bloodstream.

To an extent far greater than the ultramontanism so beloved to neoscholasticism would ever have allowed possible, the renovating churchmen succeeded in demedievalizing Catholicism on earth, which was like tearing off the healthiest, most well-developed limbs of a great oak tree. The genius that built Chartres, the genius that had perfected our liturgy and its music, was exterminated. The modern liturgy is a ghostly, bloodless abstraction compared to the richly-textured traditional liturgy that appeals to every sense in a delicate lifelong courtship and raises the mind to the God beyond all, whose Word became flesh for us men and for our salvation.

Can we be so arrogant as to believe modernity represents *progress*? Progress over the masterpiece tradition gives us? Only one year before the opening of a Council whose watchword was *aggiornamento*, Pope John XXIII cited the dire words of Pope Pius XII: "Our age is marked by a clear contrast between the immense scientific and technical progress and the fearful human decline shown by 'its monstrous masterpiece . . . transforming man into a giant of the physical world at the expense of his spirit, which is reduced to that of a pygmy in the supernatural and eternal world.'"[14] The giants of the supernatural and eternal world were the anonymous makers of the sacred liturgy, its chants and ceremonies, its vessels and vestments, its furnishings and architecture. The only sensible thing for moderns to do would be to renounce their proud *aggiornamento* and to sit still like little children in the schoolroom of medieval Christendom, becoming lifelong apprentices in its workshop of wisdom and beauty, with the hope of someday acquiring a sliver of its mastery, with, perhaps, a

---

14. John XXIII in the Encyclical *Mater et Magistra* (1961), quoting Pius XII's Christmas eve broadcast message of 1953.

renaissance to follow after several generations. And then, at last, after so much wasteful wreckovation and redundant renovation, the words of Proust, bitter as wormwood in their present inapplicability, might finally come true again, making of him an unlikely prophet: "One may say that thanks to the persistence of the same rites in the Catholic Church as also of Catholic belief in French hearts, cathedrals are not only the most beautiful monuments of our art, but also the only ones that still live their life fully and have remained true to the purpose for which they were built."

Proust's appeal, buoyant with admiration, calls to mind another eloquent petition—one from England, in the year of 1971, signed by not one artist but by fifty-six cultural figures, many of them not Catholic, and personally delivered by Cardinal Heenan to Pope Paul VI:

> If some senseless decree were to order the total or partial destruction of basilicas or cathedrals, then obviously it would be the educated—whatever their personal beliefs—who would rise up in horror to oppose such a possibility. Now the fact is that basilicas and cathedrals were built so as to celebrate a rite which, until a few months ago, constituted a living tradition. We are referring to the Roman Catholic Mass. Yet, according to the latest information in Rome, there is a plan to obliterate that Mass by the end of the current year.
>
> One of the axioms of contemporary publicity, religious as well as secular, is that modern man in general, and intellectuals in particular, have become intolerant of all forms of tradition and are anxious to suppress them and put something else in their place. But, like many other affirmations of our publicity machines, this axiom is false. Today, as in times gone by, educated people are in the vanguard where recognition of the value of tradition is concerned, and are the first to raise the alarm when it is threatened.

We are not at this moment considering the religious or spiritual experience of millions of individuals. The rite in question, in its magnificent Latin text, has also inspired a host of priceless achievements in the arts—not only mystical works, but works by poets, philosophers, musicians, architects, painters and sculptors in all countries and epochs. Thus, it belongs to universal culture as well as to churchmen and formal Christians. In the materialistic and technocratic civilization that is increasingly threatening the life of mind and spirit in its original creative expression—the word—it seems particularly inhuman to deprive man of word-forms in one of their most grandiose manifestations.

The signatories conclude by saying that "they wish to call to the attention of the Holy See, the appalling responsibility it would incur in the history of the human spirit were it to refuse to allow the Traditional Mass to survive."[15] Why appalling? Gushurst-Moore suggests a reason: "The great books of literature, history, science, mathematics, or other subjects, and the great works in the history of art or music, are very much akin to religion and faith in revealing the face of God."[16] Or, in Proust's lapidary formulation: "The clergy would be mistaken if it turned away support from artists."

One can understand why the drafter of the 1971 petition might have subscribed to the pious myth that the Holy See is capable of

---

15. For the text and annotated list of signatories, see Joseph Shaw (ed.), *The Case for Liturgical Restoration. Una Voce Studies on the Traditional Latin Mass* (Brooklyn: Angelico Press, 2019), 213–16. The response—a slender opening of permission, under strictly regimented conditions, for the old Mass, which established a precedent for ever-widening permissions in 1984 and 1988 until the fiction of a need for permission was set aside in 2007—earned the nickname "the Agatha Christie indult" because of the legend that Paul VI looked at the list of signatories and perked up when he saw her name, as he was an avid fan of her detective stories. It seems to have taken a non-Catholic writer of mysteries to make a Catholic pope allow the mysteries, in their traditional form.

16. *Glory in All Things*, 121.

"refusing to allow the Traditional Mass to survive." Today, we are in a better position to see what Agatha Christie and her cosignatories could not. As Pope Benedict XVI lucidly declared, the Church's liturgical tradition does not need the permission of any pope in order to exist or to continue to exist. The classical Roman Rite is a monument of tradition that can never be abolished, abrogated, or abandoned. The Holy Spirit Who formed this rite in the womb of Holy Mother Church would never allow such a betrayal, nor would the devoted children of that same Mother tolerate it. Cathedrals may rise and fall, revolutions ignite and subside, but this divine worship will endure until the Parousia. Proust's marveling words will never fail to be true somewhere on the face of the earth, whether it be Chartres or a cabin in the woods where a hunted priest hides: "*It still does exist* and has not really changed since the great century when the cathedrals were built."

Every age is indebted to cultural figures like Marcel Proust and Agatha Christie who have the good sense to protest ever-renewed assaults on Western civilization and the Catholic Church. But a still greater need there will always be, and a greater reward, for stubborn believers who cling to tradition and give it continual life. They will be found adoring Host and Chalice elevated above the altars of a former or future Christendom, adoring the Victor who reigns beyond the veil after all His enemies have licked the dust (Psalm 71:9). The Traditional Mass survives not by the sufferance of its overlords but by the ever-renewed love of the little ones in Christ, who, however unworthy, join centuries of pilgrims to Chartres, to the Virgin, and to the Mass, threefold image of a single heavenly Jerusalem.

Dr. Peter Kwasniewski
Feast of St. Gabriel the Archangel
March 24, 2021

ACKNOWLEDGMENTS

The first version of John Pepino's translation appeared at the weblog *Rorate Caeli* on January 13, 2015. The original French, "La Mort des cathédrales: Une conséquence du projet Briand sur la Séparation," *Le Figaro* 50 3rd ser. 229 (August 16, 1904): 3–4, is available from *Gallica* on its website at https://gallica.bnf.fr/ark:/12148/bpt6k286706d.item.

The essay by Peter Kwasniewski was published in an earlier version in *The Latin Mass* 29.2 (Summer 2020): 20–25 and online at *The Remnant* on April 28, 2020. The version contained herein has been rewritten with Proust's article in view.

CPSIA information can be obtained
at www.ICGtesting.com
Printed in the USA
BVHW010244241221
624818BV00002B/94